The Hen Can't Help It!

A first look at the life cycle of a chicken

Sam Godwin

an imprint of Hodder Children's Books

A hen sits quietly on her nest. She looks fast asleep...

...but she's not! She's concentrating.
How long has she been sitting there, Mummy?
About half an hour, dear.

Suddenly, the hen flaps her wings,
Wow, that hen lays an egg every day!

Can I touch the new egg, Mummy?

Oh no, dear. Never touch an egg or the hen won't return to her nest.

raises her tail and lays an egg!

Then the hen walks around to stretch her legs.

The cockerel brings her something to eat.
Here you are, darling. Your favourite!
Yuck!

When the hen has enough eggs in her nest,

Brooding
again, pet?
The hen sits
on her eggs
to keep them
warm.
she stops laying.

Inside each egg, a baby chicken is growing.

The yolk is the yellow part of the egg.

At first it is just a tiny speck.

Then the chick starts to grow

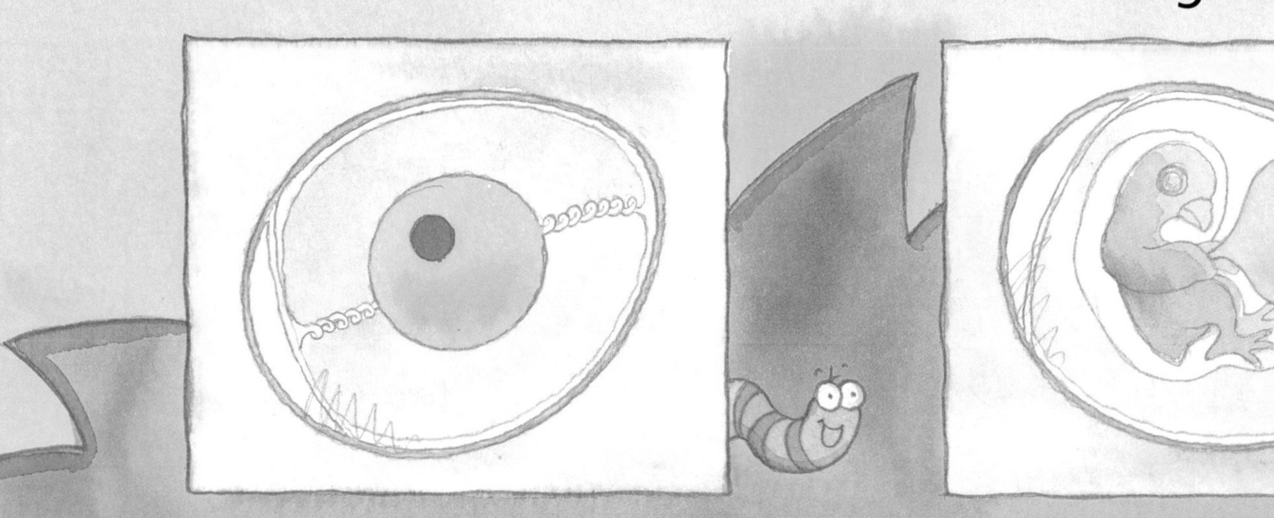

The chick is growing legs and wings and a tail. It has feathers, too.

bigger and bigger...

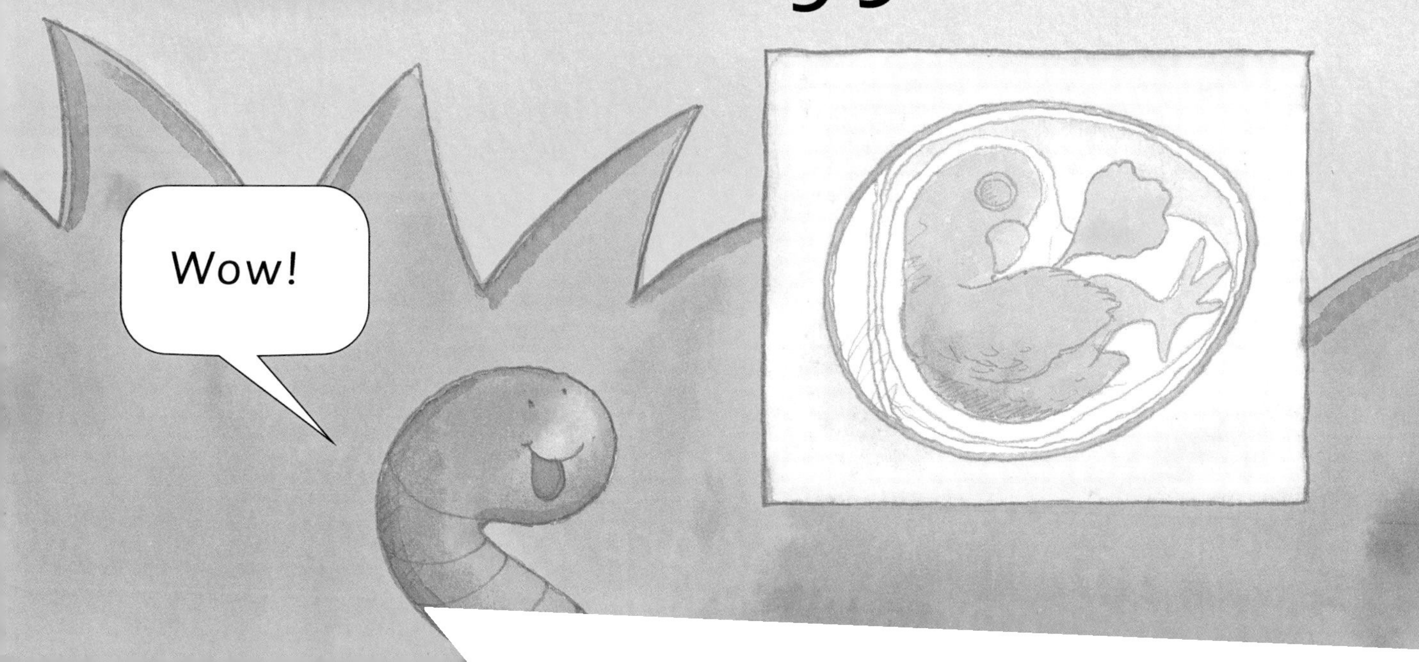

Are you OK, Hen? You've been sitting there for three whole weeks.

I'm a bit stiff, dear.

The chick also grows a sharp tip on its beak.

Why does it need
a special tip,
Mummy?
You'll see.

Darling, they're here!
Suddenly, the chicks start tapping their way

Now calm down, dear. We've been through all this before.

out of the eggs.

Ah! That's what the sharp tips on the beaks are for.

At last the chicks have hatched.

No, they have just eaten up the last of the egg yolk.

They are wet and tired from all that tapping.

My little chicks,
they're all so
eggstraordinary!

The chicks shelter under their mother's wings.

But soon they are dry and ready to play.

The chicks grow quickly. They learn to walk,

How did you get up there?
run and fly up to a perch.

Soon, the chicks grow into hens and cockerels.

I’m a granny!
Mummy, why is the hen in such a flap?
She can’t help it, dear. She’s a hen.
The hens lay eggs of their own.

Useful words

Chick
A young chicken.

Cockerel
A male adult chicken.

Hatch
To come out of an egg.

Hen
A female adult chicken.

Nest
The home of some birds, insects or other animals. Some creatures are born in the nest.

Perch
A place, such as a bar or a branch, for a bird to rest.

Yolk
A yellow sack inside an egg, full of food for the unhatched chick.